ONE WINDOW NORTH

Poetry by Kate Foley

Soft Engineering
A Year Without Apricots
Night and Other Animals
Laughter from the Hive
The Silver Rembrandt
A Fox Assisted Cure

ONE WINDOW NORTH

Kate Foley

Shoestring Press

All rights reserved. No part of this work covered by the copyright hereon may be reproduced or used in any means – graphic, electronic, or mechanical, including copying, recording, taping, or information storage and retrieval systems – without written permission of the publisher.

Printed by imprintdigital
Upton Pyne, Exeter
www.imprintdigital.net

Typset by types of light
typesoflight@gmail.com

Published by Shoestring Press
19 Devonshire Avenue, Beeston, Nottingham, NG9 1BS
(0115) 925 1827
www.shoestringpress.co.uk

First published 2012
© Copyright: Kate Foley
The moral right of the author has been asserted

ISBN 978 1 907356 63 6

ACKNOWLEDGEMENTS

Versions of some of these poems have appeared in *Ambit*, *The Amsterdam Quarterly* (online), *Artemis Poetry*, *Chroma*, *Scintilla*, *The Ver Prize 2012*, *The Poetry Salzburg Review*, the anthologies *A Twist of Malice* and *Cracking On* (Grey Hen Press, 2008 and 2009) and *This Island City: Portsmouth in Poetry* (Spinnaker Press, 2010).

Thanks to Claire and John Peasnall for the cover.

CONTENTS

How Loaves Come Singing	3
A Short Chapter in the History of Stone	4
For Agnes Sina-Imakoju	6
The Tin Factory	7
More or Less an Island	8
Three Women Smile	10
The Man Who Won't Wear Clothes	12
A Tree Thinks	13
An Oasis Outside Birmingham	14
Out of the Ark	16
To Dream of Animals	18
Wild Places	19
Tikkun Olam	20
Of Crows and Dogs	22
Please Let Me Touch the Bear	23
Tesco	24
Oh Kevin,	25
One for the Memory Palace	26
In Quaker Meeting	28
Coming in Late	29
A Perfect Rain	37
Fireman and Fox	38
One Window North	39
All the Virgins Have Come In	40
Goddesses	42
Down to Portsmouth	44
Of Mice and Bus Conductors	46
Oma	47
Waiting for Garlands	48
The Right Bones	49

Paradox	50
Postcards	51
Collecting Masterman Road	52
A Sky to Feed In	54
I Begin to Understand the Shape of Your Language	55
A Gift of Rivers	56
To the Field of Reeds	57
Heart Surgery	58
Prince Rupert's Drops	59
One Shoe Dropped	60
When	61
A Different Ceremony	62
The Cardinal in his Birthday Suit	63
One Sunday Smiling in the Vondel Park	66
Binding the Word	68
A Poem is not a Jug	69

For Tonnie Bakkenist with love

HOW LOAVES COME SINGING

Those who are statistically a little closer
to death, not necessarily wise,
are less inclined

to find the idea romantic.
Instead, knowing how far we've come
we look at the news

with a kind of desperate sorrow
we dare not waste on ourselves.
This one wrapped in a white sheet.

That one broken.
Every morning we remember
how loaves come singing out of the oven,

how there is always
one bird
that misses the shaken tablecloth.

A SHORT CHAPTER IN THE HISTORY OF STONE

Small girls play in the shadow of mud brick walls.
A pile of jackstones flips from grubby palm
to sharp knuckle.

Dreaming, nursing stone babies –
some have gold flecks in their round heads,
like the sun in a pail of water.

Pebble in a first pair of grown-up
shoes. His parents. Yours. You kick off the hot
fidgety shoe secretly under your robe.

Your brother burns flags. Throws unerring stones
at embassy cars. Skips home
like a young goat.

Your first child is a girl.
You make a leaf bracelet
for her chubby wrist.

Not very old yourself
you try to soften the rock-hard disapproval
of your not very old husband

who will never believe
his sperm has selected two
baby girls.

One burnt supper. One tearful wife
runs from the compound leaving a smell
of scorch in the air,

holds her swollen cheek, trips on a stone,
falls in the gravelly dust, is lifted
by a friend of her brother,

who runs his thumb gently over her eyelids.
The rest will soon be history
written by stone.

FOR AGNES SINA-IMAKOJU

(aged 16 and shot in a take-away)

Pity is not a big enough container
for a dead girl. All tomorrow
won't fit and even yesterday
spills. Messages wilt
on supermarket bouquets.
'Loveya always' when 'never'
in a painstaking hand
is still too many light years away
from those who twin it with 'forget.'

A small bright bead of DNA,
she might have worn it in her hair,
has rolled out of sight.

Millions of years of evolution
led to the intelligent flex of the finger
that belonged to the boy who will always
be clemmed in his starved matchbox
of leftover living, whose frantic feet
in too big trainers can't run him away
from their unlived lives, hers, his.

THE TIN FACTORY

where I have been fitted with a new heart
rustles like the rattle of corrugated roofs
heard from a distance.

A great many people are waiting there,
since a heart of flesh
confers no evolutionary advantage.

You have to be braver
than most of us are
to wear one.

We don't look
at each other or ask
what are our eyes made of?

At this, the cheaper end of the market,
tick tock is not digitized.
You have a small key

in your back.
Sometimes – a design flaw –
the stressed metal of your heart

will see a sight that makes it scream
like a burnt baby. Up to you
what you do with the key.

MORE OR LESS AN ISLAND

From Peter Pan: *J. M. Barrie*

Oma sits, one end of the birthday table,
Opa at the other, both facing the same way.

A daughter to the left and one across,
one son-in-law with Tintin quiff,

one gelled. They josh her but she only smiles
when Peking duck overflows her plate,

when grandchild sets a small hand on her knee
and chocolates come with china tea.

Nobody knows what Oma thinks
and if she does how repartee sounds in her head –

like fireworks crackling? Graceful
waiters bend at the waist.

They light a sparkler, play a birthday song.
She stares them through and hugs her plate.

She doesn't flicker as we sing.

But when we come to leave
she strains the tablecloth through fingers

tight as unoiled hinges,
her stranded Easter Island face adrift.

A waiter catches as she staggers,
turns her deftly as a jelly from its mould

into her wheelchair, where Opa waits.
Facing the same way.

THREE WOMEN SMILE

Platonov: '…the world grows its heart from your ugliness'

Three women smile
at each other on the train.
I lost my face somewhere.

Pigeons clap the glass roof
and rain falls on the platform.
'…the world grows its heart

from your ugliness.' Really?
I don't know what I look like
anymore.

Homemade pigeon-clouds
dapple the face
of the woman

asleep with a book
in her lap. She feels
them like leaves.

She is grey, untidy.
Her face opens with sheer
good humour.

As she smiles
the woman in the hijab
across the aisle

sees my own face
smile back. Tired
creases in her skin

blaze softly. I smile again.
I may not be growing heart
but for now I have found my face.

THE MAN WHO WON'T WEAR CLOTHES

– especially in prison,
where dyed in the vat of other men's dreams
they're stiff as communal winding sheets –
sits naked and stringy,
pale as a stick of celery,
in the cell of himself.

Once, every few years
he passes through the scarred gates
and feels the wind the magistrates can't forbid
in the crack where his soul waits.

Thank you man – some say you're mad
as a bag of cats – for knowing
how masks can be complicit,
for insisting
on bare.

A TREE THINKS

First the smallest of root hairs twitches,
looses hold on a crumb of earth, nudges

its neighbour. Soon, deep underground countless
rootlets seethe like a football crowd,

that breathless moment before a goal.
On the long travel between root and crown

a tree talks to itself. Deep as a beehive
sound resonates, sings small songs

through cracks in bark so
pinpoint insects hear,

glow with effort, carry the bolus of hum
in their mouths.

Trees are not tyrants,

they know the cost of messages
but they are building toward birds.

Darlings of the deep space between,
birds will never drop

the weighty thoughts of trees.
Not while there's breath and feather.

AN OASIS OUTSIDE BIRMINGHAM

A tongue of green
between two lips of desert.

Birmingham over there.
He had a tree once,

misses the shade. And a goat.
God! She was tough.

But the water still comes – have they forgotten it? –
seeping through an aging root system

of pierced plastic, courtesy of the civil servant
in charge of Bio-diversity Fostering Nodules.

That's him. He's a BDFN.
He does invertebrates.

Every month a tired old plane heaves itself
out of the sky,

shrugs its rusty shoulders,
sulks down

on his swept asphalt.
Every month there is less of everything.

The labels on the tins look tireder
and he dare not ask *what about soap?*

or tinned peas? Coffee
belongs to the poetics of memory.

Every month he struggles to open his mouth
to the cured-leather tortoise

of a pilot to ask w*hat if?...when?*
He manages *OK? Ticking over out there?*

A deep rust has mercifully corroded
the roots of both their tongues.

Every day he makes meticulous notes about tumorous ants
in ant-sized writing.

He would like to be able to die before the distant blue of
                                                                 Birmingham

stops reminding of rain.

OUT OF THE ARK

twobytwo bytwo bytwo bytwo
the boat fills, spilled from the old toybox.

Battered creatures multiply
like the silk-lined rabbits

who hop softly aboard.
An elephant lumbers up the gangplank

shipped out from a corner of the room,
domestic cats learn from paw prints

of their feral elders, little dogs
wear flashy neckerchiefs,

monkeys snatch our fitful
attention and snicker, a tall

giraffe sees further
than ever we wanted,

and cows whose quiet rumble of digestion
and milk

speaks field and kitchen
may bring tears.

Don't even think about the mythical beasts
who shuffle below the waterline

or the birds

who cling like blossom to the rig
but may fly away.

How to move all that weight,
that freight with the twin oars

of memory and sleep, to drag the ship
with only the psalm of our hands?

TO DREAM OF ANIMALS

is musk and straw, the slow tick of an egg
and blood slipping through your heart, heavy
as dressed silk.

Barrelling down waterfalls of wind a chimp
flies and cows, their marigold-glove
udders comfortably empty after milking,
are silos of stillness.

To dream of animals only seems like a blessing.
They don't bless. Fitting company
for the first shadowless light of earth,
their simple shadows

are patches of missing sunlight. Nothing more,
while ours are crusted, barnacled,
stiff, not to be laid down even in sleep,
where sometimes the ghosts

of our virtual selves allow a dream.

WILD PLACES

Flesh hangs from his neck like an alderman's chains.
Sky flocks for him. White cows mill the ground.
Swinging his stones in their smooth leather pouch
he strolls to the water tank. Horns thick and short
as a builder's fingers, he butts a drinking cow,
looks up, sees us, licks the folds of the cow's behind,
pounds the ground once and grins like a minotaur.

I think of all the girls with chipped red toenails
and pearly lips, their breath jostling, elbows
and knees out, running to the wild places,
not knowing
that even the pavements aren't tame.

TIKKUN OLAM

mending the world

Season of jars and bottles when foetal plums
curl in on themselves, a bloodknot, rich on kitchen shelves,

when apples blaze like emperors,
when there are leaves on the line.

Though the cropped lion's ruff in fields
suggests a yield that never came,

because the Crack of Doom's so slow,
you can forget the scruffy bees

that rub their balding bodies
on scanty pollen while pigeons inch

on crippled feet.
You'd rather sweep out on a clean tsunami

with blackened fag-end flies, stained plastic,
disembowelled tvs

but now the virtual plastic of the Stock Exchange
in domino effect means Footsie's fall's

the only wave you'll get. Season of fruit
whose colours lend decay

romance, the world's wound stinks
like a bird in the chimney.

Mending is no hero's task. Think
instead, raw threads, cobbled patches,

tear-stained, blood-stained needle pricks
and where it's rotten fabric parts

a patient, industrious makeover
of the heart.

OF CROWS AND DOGS

Such lewd, ungainly birds, humping the air.
Grounded, they waddle like pantomime dames.

But dogs bundle up their back legs against their chests,
then *chocks away!*

unroll the ribbon of themselves. Both laugh.
Dogs silently with deep throated intention.

Crows concentrate sarcasm, black as a jar
of marmite. And yes, yes, YES, of course whales

must be saved but yesterday I saw a tiny bantam hen
march peaceably in feathered trousers

on the warm back
of a pregnant goat.

PLEASE LET ME TOUCH THE BEAR

after reading Liliana Ursu

I don't know who I'm asking
only that the dark fur,
raveled at the edge with light
speaks more prayer
than any candle

and its feet, bigger than dinner plates,
flap and bang the earth
as if they were cousins.

Let me come close enough
to dare bear spit,
bright teeth, ravenous arms
and touch.

Let me for once, if only once,
ignore the Health and Safety legislation
and feel that spark
travel up my arm.

You speak of your best cinnamon years.
Don't you see why fresh footprints, scat
and a glowing tuft of tail hair,
can never be enough?

I won't take no for an answer.
I must touch the bear.

TESCO

angels like apples
        rolling from a tree

must wash their faces
        calculate their body-mass index

there are to be
        no more unawares

        no more visitors
with luminous footprints

        no wings in the aisles

the cash registers will whisper
        not ring now that paper

the secret voice of trees
        is disappearing

        send me a sign
a scab on the skin

of my potato
        a bruise on my apricot

        let there be chicken bottom fluff
stuck to my egg

OH KEVIN,

(Apologies to Bill Manhire)

Bill says we have to go
at last into the radio.
Is it true?

        Oh!

So dark in there you have to find
your way by the keen of knobs
sweeping a pointer

over a half-lit dial
and broken-biscuit crumbs
of tiny voices

spit hissy static from
behind the thick gold screen.
Now all those heavy radios

squat in museums,
their voices shuffled together,
old cards from a busted flush.

You want to be Heritage,
Kevin? Not me.
I'm straight up the chimney

like a scorched lark
into the thin forgettable air
away from the dark.

ONE FOR THE MEMORY PLACE

A birthday. Where we are today.

Amsterdam's best Dim Sum, waiters sweating black and white,
dark wooden food-wheel rocking as spattered cuffs reach.
Leaf-wrapped parcels.

A Chinese pair lean together like willow leaves after
a long conversation.

Their child, their small ivory,
sucks his comforter,
his baby punk black silk quills
fanned on his pillow.

A small, square, buzz-cut boy, his prehensile thumb gaming.
His other hand shoots out like a piston for food.
His ears prick. A thread of sound, a baby mew.
Swift as a little tug-boat he's under the table.
Up and out of sight, he rocks the pram. Unseen, he thinks,
he strokes the covers straight.

The mother plucks her parcelled child from his blanket,
his lashes wet calligraphy on his cheeks,
while our boy – for he must belong to us all, to look at a child
with such tenderness that every battered piece
in the Memory Palace glows – crawls back under the table
to his game, his place,
his Dim Sum.

O let him keep
such kindness.

But this, after all, is Amsterdam, where grown men
ride battered pink bikes, hung with plastic flowers.

He's in with a chance.

IN QUAKER MEETING

When he wakes
          to find himself in the transparent air of meeting
the old man's smile reflects the inverse curve of his painful back.
          Old women sit, their hands like root vegetables.
Their laps are at peace.
          Surely we all have the same secrets
locked between our thighs, the same shabby bald spots
          on the nap of love or action?

Goodness rises like cream, skimmed by the light.
          Give me some of that I want to say
but there is no-one to ask and only
          the plain light from the windows,
the small scrunch and shift
          of elderly bones on a bench.

COMING IN LATE

1. Rehearsal

Poised as a heron, he raises his hands
cloaked in old skin folded over
his wrists.

HUP! He rises on a singing note.
Heron to frog, a scissor-legged
leap.

Music breaks out of its tight bud.
The bellies of plump-lipped putti swell.
Chandeliers drop notes.

The boy on the drums
with haystack hair pours out
a thunderous barrel of apples.

Violins bend from the waist
pulled by the bow
and flutes

open their gills in clear water.
We have shuffled in
out of the boring weather

to watch this building site of sound
go up, to pass the time
before the time

is past. But as the violin's wood
remembers every bee,
we practice

involuntary
wax and honey
in the vaulted dark.

2. A Short prehistory of music

He wants them to leave the rolling, schubertian uplands,
to titillate the notes, mozartify the landscape, put a skip
in the little hills of music.

They want stately.
They're used to it.
But he's boss.

Suddenly he cracks the right joke.
Eyebrows lower.
Mouths relax.

His hand, trembling a little, casts the lure.
Tiny hawk notes fly round, dive, settle on his wrist.
Both hands now scatter the tempo like corn.

*didididididi***DAH** ....the cellist leans so far in
his yarmulka flaps like a teapot lid
while double bassists power high shoulders forward,
synchronised swimmers.

He gentles the air, a downward pat,
and beckons the wind.

The first people blew on rocks,
made tenor hills, far off pizzicato mountains

      the silence in between.

They say now the world is made from words
but that's only the half
of it, isn't it?

3. We were late when we came in

We chose to ignore the man outside with flowers in his hat
shouting 'choose for Jesus.'

We chose instead free coffee, the susurration of silk and tweed
on velvet seats.

We chose the bullring. Today's heavy, many-headed bull
baited and wooed with a baton.

We may not roar.
We have no role.
Our role is not to take part.

We are getting anxiously older by the minute. Banderillas fly –
                                                     one gets
an oboist, square in his arpeggio   while *DAAAaaagrrr***UP**
goes straight to the midriff of the double bass
who lifts his great whale-bodied instrument over his head,
then sets it gently down.

Standoff. The man with the baton lays it on his book,
places his hands together in prayer, lifts his stick again and in
                                                    a silence
ringing with entreaty, gestures the flutes.
Their notes glide out like a woman sliding forward her elegant
                                                         shoe.

When the bull roars with one voice, we are not prepared
for our longing to take part in that glorious melancholy.
O let us, *do* let us – but it's not going to happen
anymore than god is going to share his daisies.

We were old when we came in
because that is what we do with our time
but at least we have been rehearsing.

4. Tears are appropriate for this piece

A young pianist, wobbly as a calf,
her plump fingers butting the notes,
tears on her face.

Fish don't cry. Their fluid skin
keeps the tears of ocean out.
Not deer, stitching through the dapple of death,
nor birds, stiff as clothes pegs
in the mouths of cats,
none of them cry
and we are sometimes very mean indeed
with our species-specific gift.

When we come to do the sums,
what did we ever do to deserve it,
to be able to cry
my words, yours,
the music?

5. We are saying our prayers

in the concert hall, devout faces
bent over our Blackberry screens,
blue lights flashing on naked cherubs,
our agile thumbs worshipping.

We enter a period of fasting, prescribed
by the management, a dose of unadulterated music.
Black suited men and draped women sway,
singing in their strings
and their fluted breath

but Orfeo-Orfea –

>   who has long forgotten
>   why or what or whose
>   is the face broken
>   behind the beard,
>   sliver of the god he was,
>   glimpsed in a shop window,
>   sherd of the goddess,
>   collected in a plastic bag of notes,

– flies in,

leaves the Roma
sitting with his sax on the pavement,
the dark old woman with her tired
tambourine.
            Can you hear?

>   The cry of urban foxes
>   is burnt into their song,

the rocks are groaning
on their knees,

trees would walk
remembering
on their bleeding
roots
if they could,

the planet is saying *love?*
this is death I weep for…

and with our glass of free wine
in the interval and our deprived thumbs
we are only mildly sorry, after the final applause,
to click on our phones.

6. If we could make you like a poem, god

or music,
then we'd owe each other nothing.

It was you, wasn't it, who first said that music
must be kept in its box of notes and that words
mustn't run, bump into each other,
jump the queue?

But the first poem made room
for the solitary song of breath on a blade of grass
the high caterwaul of storm
the tiny unheard click as beads of DNA come together
on the same string.

You have got above yourself.

How did you escape, fly into orbit,
choose Star Wars over the old unspoken rites
when we made you and you made us new?

I see my thumb print on your face,
my label in your collar,
your heavy comb scratches my parting straight.

Shall we stop now? Shall we spill the music
out of the cup of its making? Shall we let the words
out of their striped pyjamas?

Sing, maybe?

A PERFECT RAIN

('the lit bush' from The Bright Field*: R. S. Thomas)*

Imagine the past. Isn't that what we do?
Lay down trace after trace of cobweb remembering.
Even the rip that runs transverse
to all we think is written in our blood only exists
because we dream it does.
The perfect rain falls down
and building is what creatures
do, a smear of clay,
a past,
a patiently fitted twig.
Few can praise
the lit bush
for what it is,
simply transfigured by a morning.

FIREMAN AND FOX

Rabbits sleep
like old shoes
in their burrows.

Old couples, one
half of a pair
of inverted commas, snore.

In the sidings
freight trains
click their cooling metal hides

and everyone,
everything – tables, chairs
spoons – is asleep.

I have taken my head off and put it
in the fridge where its gelid glare sees
feisty cheese, ravaged butter, a sausage

with a secret life. I will not
not think of women exhorted to push,
people in cardboard boxes, prisoners, a child.

I envy those like the fireman
and the fox whose duty it is
to stay awake.

Morning is a cliché I refuse.
There is no last line.

ONE WINDOW NORTH

Two windows in this room.
Southwards in early morning
roofs blaze apocalyptic silver,

a chestnut tree runs
medieval green and gold
and scruffy garden hedges

flash like spokes of a wheel.
Then I turn my back on the south,
and while the coffee creaks in its pot

look north.
It's there where the bricks
are plain serviceable oblongs

for holding in, where the sober
roof tiles only contain
and the grey pavement

doesn't sparkle,
that the true north is made
for planting your feet.

ALL THE VIRGINS HAVE COME IN

and taken up their places in the museum
on glass shelves
in long rows
one after the other, after the other.

Each has a little boy baby, each achieves
therefore, what women
should,
lucky, lucky long-skirted virgins.

From the chunky, rough hewn twelfth
century to
the rococo,
smiling or weeping they seem comfortable

in their borrowed power from god
and the master carver,
armies
of them stuffed with a piquant male

fantasy of prayer. Look over your shoulder
at all the tortured
Christs,
their sufferings so elegantly drawn, as if

suffering is the dandyish option, an elite
occupation. Then
quickly
turn back to the virgins. Was that a foot withdrawn

under a cloak? Is that ineffable smile a tinge
ironic? See, that one?
there –
I swear she spanked Him – and that one

cries real tears of fury and frustration
over her dead
son's
wasted breath. An escaped smile, a small, weary

hint of reality in lip or cheek, even the man
with the chisel, dreaming
of Jesus
can't negate the power of all the virgins coming in.

GODDESSES

They belong to their faces
as only those

who've become the landscape of their skins,
                                            belong.

They belong to their breasts,
reach casually into their bras,

feed peevish businessmen, a dying child,
a distempered dog, headmistresses,

the odd dictator.

Often asked for forgiveness
or other impossible things,

they look at penitents
and petitioners steadily,

as a gift. No return is asked
or expected.

They belong to their bellies,
relish a digestif of sly chuckles

and fat peals of laughter, dirty
as soapsuds when a job is done.

Appetite, old friend, is known
biblically, met in the pleasure
                                of pleasing.

They belong to their wombs
only as those who are sure

the seed case is not the seed
and the root hair not the soil.

Ordinary as a Tesco tillroll
they belong to their deaths

as utterly as fading comes
and one collapsing star feeds another.

Fortunately,
there are very many more of them
                                   than you think.

DOWN TO PORTSMOUTH

Miss Powell had thick legs.
Neighed like a carthorse.
She did the Infants
so you never noticed how glossy
her mane was when she laughed.

Miss Thomas was little and spry.
Like a bird you'd think but boy!
she had a tongue on her to shave wood.
Lumping great kids at the Elementary
ate from her hand.

Down from Wales to Portsmouth,
came to do their bit.
Bombs flew like turnips
thumped in the back of a cart,
torn paper wildfires crackled.

Fireweed, they called that rash of purple
on the bomb sites. Used to make
Miss Thomas and Miss Powell think
of proper flowers. Used to make
that tough little madam

Miss Thomas cry and Miss Powell
stroke the back of her neck
with a gruff hand. Neat
as a pin, their two rooms.
Good china. Found a chip, later,

with mauve flowers you could
see through. *Shame…*
said the fireman after the bomb.
*blast must've blown their nighties
right off…*

clasped together… *naked
as the day they were born.…*

OF MICE AND BUS CONDUCTORS

Grazing the deep yellow fog
amber light from a blazing torch.
Streaks of scarlet climb like sepsis
in an infected arm. The bus conductor,
cap visor low, leads his lumbering
double-decker,
              both coughing.
The folds of fog rumble with coughs,
ripe, fruity, then harsh as your tongue
on the pit of a plum. It drapes
round your shoulders, dribbles
down your neck. Your father
coughs, tugs your mother. She tugs
you, a small flotilla,
              all coughing.
We trip on a granite kerb,
feel paving stones tilt to our blind
feet. The ironmongers broad window
glows dim as a dying bulb. Heaped
sacks of grass seed, a mower, shears
and running like live silk a river
of mice. Freshets
              of bright eyes,
ears pricked as the crest
of a wave, whiskers flicked like midges
on skin. Sealed in their globe
of faint light they are as present
to their world as you are other
to them – the whole night
              stained with light,
echoing with coughs
and the patient, steel capped ring
of bus conductors' feet.

OMA

I'm my own grandmother.
How? I'm no believer

but every time I open my door
and pass those two caryatids, Love and Kindness

standing in the hall, I touch their worn
marble hems prayerfully.

Where once I failed to love my mirror,
now I see light and threads the Norns have spun,

or might – a canny harvesting of sun,
a shine from other faces, shadow

threads, a leading dark that stitches me
my proper place.

Mothers? I've put them to bed with my dolls,
but tenderly, older now,

still in need of my own forgiveness
though not of theirs. And the child?

Harder. Some children have such very old, small faces
shrink-wrapped in sorrow.

Only the grandmother of time
can lay a finger on their cheeks.

WAITING FOR GARLANDS

Ancestors, a faint trace,
the quizzical lift of an eyebrow,
a fade in the mirror.

They're not solid black marble,
gilded v-cut alphabets
or corroded letters –

more a scrambled SMS.

Ancestors are shy,
won't presume connection.
They flit on the edge of memory,

a stain like a moth's wing clapped shut
in the family bible,
a lingering smell,

coffee? drains? the room you lost it in?
skin? – closest of all molecular keys
opening the loved to the lost.

They are not who your mother told you you were.

Neglected household gods in their niches,
they squat, longing to answer
unspoken prayers,

waiting for garlands.

THE RIGHT BONES

'Where do birds usually go to die?' you ask
'Is there somewhere like an elephants' graveyard?'

A passing car or cat got this one.
Its down jacket must still be warm.

Quills are still oil-slick bright, upstanding
but the ruby eyes are dull little gravels

and the coral feet a crippled grey.
Somebody, imitating the reticent

decency of the way birds like to die
has swept it into a doorway.

I imagine a bird feeling its pulse fail,
settling its last warmth

on the I Ching puzzle of ancestor bones
folding not-needed wings

round the small leaves of its feet,
quietly letting the migratory knot

in its forehead fade.
I would like that too

one day
if only I can find the right bones.

PARADOX

'Mirror, mirror on the wall'
the old joke says
'I am my mother after all'

but which?

Feathers, grain, eggs, fluff.
I had two mothers once.
More than enough.

A red hen and a white,
two mothers once.
One stayed and one took flight.

The red laid eggs that broke.
The white flew off
to avoid the yoke.

Not before time in grace
of mirror light a third appears.
Late and slow I learn her face.

Feathers, grain, eggs, fluff.
Three mothers now.
More than enough.

POSTCARDS

Slumbering on my mantelpiece
the Fat Lady from a Maltese tomb.

She doesn't have to prove anything
or ever wake up.

Heaped as a croissant.
whatever caused her to lie down forever

has left only a trace of red
ochre. Her neighbour,

the Hooded Lady, carved from the horn
of an unimaginable beast,

no longer smokes with cold
or listens to the bone flute

play a tune we'll never know
if we've remembered

or reinvented.
Stone tools or pixels.

Tracks of long dead silences.
A bell ringing underwater.

COLLECTING MASTERMAN ROAD

Black fists of pollarded planes punch above their weight
in shadows,
knob-heads shaved, scabs from their last tattoo
peeling.
      In the Jewish graveyard stones gleam like apologetic teeth.

Bells do their holy-metal arpeggios for nobody much.
This is not for you… This is not for you. On a rising scale I hear
                                                                                that swing
in the park where the rooks crook their hooded elbows,
pinching each other's twigs.

I collect

X1 kid in a toy police car
wheeuw wheeuw
x2 dogs
who serially lift their legs
x1/2 a foil bottle top
x 1000s of buds fat as mealworms
wriggling to a different tune
than the bells intend.

I note

so many colours in the stain of sadness
soft as sun on brick,
I don't know the number of her house anymore.
Love and forgetting leave prints
and hollows in the space they stood.

I place

The morning's absence
of elegy
labelled
on this shelf of days.

A SKY TO FEED IN

may be eye blue or blue as the shadow
on a bone,

need not be without cloud.
Your face grows its prehistory hour by hour,

one eye slightly triangular as are the eyes of all
beautiful women,

the other, scooped out, pearlised as a shell or the tender
luminescent inside of a shucked bean pod.

When I first knew you, I didn't bargain for that alchemical hour
with the white-coated eye maker

fusing his blue black and crimson rods in white heat
to fine threads,

getting the colour matched to the every day, worn
slightly faded sky

you can hold in your hand, intimate
as the inside of a mouth,

didn't know how soon I would find myself
coiled as a warm cat

in the deep still-life of your wisest eye.

I BEGIN TO UNDERSTAND THE SHAPE OF YOUR LANGUAGE

how it curls up asleep in your mouth.
Did you know you snore in Dutch?

I'm beginning to speak pictogram,
hieroglyph, crotchets and quavers

and see how I never understood the 8 bar rest
is part of the music.

I'm glad of the dark, that shelf of flotsam,
where I watch daylight rub

your profile to silver on its sleeve.
Your mouth opens with a soft plof!

All the fat nouns and athletic verbs stretch.
My hearing aid is out

so I shall only hear them buzz.
No matter. All night the soft conversation

of cells meanders, teaching fluency
in the branched tributaries of my heart.

A GIFT OF RIVERS

Flying into Amsterdam
I see how a giant comb has pulled the hairs of the fields
into straight, wet lines, how the occasional hedge
runs on wiry feet away from the open,
                                      how as the plane tilts
the edge of the water-land-water seems ghostly as the meniscus
an empty glass has left behind,
                                  how the many transparent
voices of water thicken in canals
and the old windows in the city
are so like rolled water you wait for fish
to swim through their bubbles.

When I left the branches across our yard
were empty. Now small green fists
punch out space.

Thank you for your gift of rivers.

TO THE FIELD OF REEDS

The heart is measured in a scale against the feather in the Egyptian Book of the Dead

42 gods waiting,
a placard held up,
one for each sin.

My heart, fat, elderly, shabby,
surely deserves some credit for keeping on
keeping on?

Over there the Field of Reeds.
My heart gives a little shall-I-make-it? skip.
Your feather trembles. Ever since I said I'm a liar

and a coward and you said yes, but I love you
I've borrowed your compass.
Now that 42 pairs of eyes

are sizing up my canopic heart,
measuring the equilibrium of the scales,
I need it.

OK, OK, myth and procrastination.
You know and I know the Field of Reeds
is nothing more or less

than a Sunday morning in our bed
while we can. But lend me your feather
and I'll look very hard for my own.

One feather on each side
trimmed and steady
as she goes.

HEART SURGERY

My right leg slung over that elegant notch
where your hip rises
canted like a western saddle,

your head parked so your ear
makes a sharp, fossil impression
in the soft of my arm,

while our more primitive, forgotten feet
flipper innocently
at the bottom of the bed.

We are for now, a many armed goddess,
a *bonne bouche* in the mouth of our planet.
We are while we can

the biological knot of a new creature
brought forward from Kells
and our multi-chambered heart

moves the breath of our blood
with such kindness
it could stop war and famine.

But printed through the DNA we share
is notice posted of that surgery
that will pare our ventricles apart.

Such elegant thrift, to let us drift with fallen winds
and ancient trace of sun
in the unswept strata of that older heart.

PRINCE RUPERT'S DROPS

(Prince Rupert used to press apparently stable glass drops into the hands of his courtiers and with a flick of his fingers they'd explode)

Heart, sober shape of raindrops,
Prince Rupert moment, poised
forever on the edge of shatter

resisting risk,
pain, funny stories that might propagate cracks,
or love – a stimulant too far.

Inside the dark red, almost black
box where you sit displayed
on wet velvet, is a new hum.

Is this, like the aftermath of the Prince's fingers,
to be the ultimate joke? One sharp tweak,
an explosion of fragments?

Rock a little Heart, pullulate,
vibrate, while you can still hear the tender
amazement of human voices and bees.

ONE SHOE DROPPED

Two shoes make conversation.
Toes turned towards each other
may speak diffidence.

Or one balanced behind its partner heel
might signify laid-back elegance.
Scuffed or shiny? tidy laces? leather

soft as worn cloth? bunion bulges?
You spot little clues
that shoes are the microphones of feet.

How then to read one lost shoe,
Square root of one
deprived of two,

it is last and emblem
for our pilgrim feet.

WHEN

the plain light fades
to a memory of light

and you can't find its root
which was only ever in you,

I don't want the gentle hands of strangers to lift you.
I want it to be me that cups

your head, so your skull nests
and your neck shivers like a tiny sigh of satisfaction.

This is what old is, when every leaf is as new as the last
and the poplars are bronzed as young helmets.

Only open, I say to my empty hand,
only open.

A DIFFERENT CEREMONY

Rust and fire,

red root of darkness, branched artery of rock,
black as the hardened tip of a throwing spear.

Bison dance a thunderous jig to death,
stately and graceful as a falling building.

Dumb as the still mouths of baby girls
littered on hillsides, death tries

with all its mimetic power to show
that falling is not done to the leaf –

it knows best how. If we could trust
that weightless fall in air, glassy as the good

stream not answerable to stop or go,
that carries us anyway, then Theseus

could swing the Minotaur into a waltz
and the ceremonies of death might be different.

THE CARDINAL IN HIS BIRTHDAY SUIT

Sitting comfortably in his oldest cassock.
Just said mass in the convent chapel.
No red sash or skull cap today.

No one can enjoy English coffee.
He does his best and likes the marmalade –
buttery fingers make little transparent windows
in *The Times* ironed by the nuns
who say it's best for a Prince of the Church,
although he's foreign
and retired.

He reads:

97% of bees already extinct.

Belgian nuns accused of sexual abuse…

WHAT?!? Men, yes!
those awkward, hinged,
sly, troubled, trousered,
self-justifying hybrids…

but these are *women* like Our Lady – and his mother was
most of the time.

And the bees, least silly of God's creatures,
working their silky way
into the soft fanny of flowers,
only building food, not empires. He knows.
He did bees once in a monastery garden.

Our fault, our fault a great bronze challenge
shakes the belfry of his throat.

The ivory beach-boy Christ on the wall
flashes his ribs and is silent.

He knows he must run through the Streets of Harlesden
crying *Woe Woe*,
he must climb the pulpit in Our Lady's church
and preach whales, bees
and the very, very small.

Quick as his stiff fingers can,
his suite of buttons fly open,
he steps out of his neat, nun-mended
long johns and wheezing, his shoes.

Chicken-skin naked he trots down the waxed hall,
past Our Lady, who gives him an old fashioned look,
past Sister Imelda, come for the dishes – **Jeeezuz**
Mary an' Joseph – past the Dragon Nun who
keeps the door – she faints.
Game as a water bird, high-stepping
on his arthritic knees,
he's out.

Crownhill road, empty. Highstreet
bobbing with shoppers – white, brown, black,
a moving tray of Belgian chocolates – **Ahhhh!**
No breath for consonants. Only a wail
edged with fury and grief.

He sees a stall lit with oranges.
'Where from?' he gasps. 'Kenya, man.'
Over they go, flashing fragrant in the gutter,
pulped under a number 18 bus.

Mobiles blink, 999, a maniac on the loose,
quick as you like – nevah there when you want'm…
a broken umbrella, he hurples, laughter strung out behind him
like ribbons from a deflating balloon.

'No identification' the Duty Sergeant smirks.
'Not circumcised, no distinguishing marks….
DO-YOU-SPEAK-ENGLISH? WHERE'JEW COME FROM?'

He drops his grey police blanket
and naked again, signs the air,

'Bliss you, my son, my dear.'

ONE SUNDAY SMILING IN THE VONDEL PARK

all the little dogs
are yanking the leads
of their people
      men whirr lycra
legs rakishly on racers
        old women in nylon tights
on oma bikes
place neat bunches
of visiting flowers
in their baskets
      skaters zip and unzip
perfect parabolas
      a middle-aged
couple contentedly
slurps ice-cream
      dreadlocks
shaved heads
    a whiff
of dope   smoke
from the skinny fire
where boys fry
sausages   a toy car
runs like a ferret
in the grass

and it is late September

so sweet and clapped
as a bell full of summer

        why
should this day ringing
with tiny accumulations of joy
not take precedence over the equinox,
when the rose no longer able to open the night
has blown out?

BINDING THE WORD

sadness feels like a pebble in your mouth
a word that won't dissolve

you can always suck it to get water
        but
is there a good word for 'joy'?
such a titchy, prim three-letter figleaf
for creatureliness
        dailyness
the fat peace of your belly after food
skin in all its phases from flesh of flower
        to vellum
with its wholesome day job
of keeping things in
        and out
and sometimes
the grasshopper leap
        of that clown the spirit

the longer I sit in the gradual fossilization of my bones
the more I know there is no substitute
for the right sadness
gilt-edged speckled and foxed
binding the word for joy you can't get hold of
into the mystery of its genes

A POEM IS NOT A JUG

or a young horse
rolling in a field of apples

      is it

how the music is a net
letting out more than it keeps in?

how a painter stands
away from the brush?

      is it

something to pour
something to contain?